JOSEPH HAYDN

SYMPHONY No. 87

A major / A-Dur / La majeur
Hob. I:87
"Paris No. 6"

Edited by/Herausgegeben von
H.C. Robbins Landon

T0081271

Ernst Eulenburg Ltd

London · Mainz · Madrid · New York · Paris · Tokyo · Toronto · Zürich

Symphony No. 87, in A major (1785)

This work was placed as No. 87 in the chronological list of 104 symphonies by E. von Mandyczewski; as such it represented the last of the six symphonies which Haydn was commissioned to write for the Parisian organization, *Les Concerts de la Loge Olympique*. At the time (1907) when this chronological position was established the autograph of this work, as well as those of Nos. 83 and 85, were not known to Haydn scholars. The subsequent discovery, by Jens Peter Larsen[1] of the holograph MSS. of Nos. 83 and 87 showed that Mandyczewski's order needed correction. It was assumed that, like the other works existing in autograph, both of these symphonies were composed in the year 1786; but the autographs of Nos. 83 and 87 are both dated 1785, showing that they should precede No. 82, the " first " of the Paris symphonies in Mandyczewski's list. In discussing the order of these six works, no one appears to have taken into consideration Haydn's letter to his publishers, Artaria (Vienna), on the subject. In this important document, dated August 2, 1787, Haydn writes[2]:—

I forgot last time to put down the order of the symphonies, which must be engraved in the following way: The Sinfonia in A [G.A. No. 87] No. 1; in B flat [No. 85] No. 2; in G minor [No. 83] No. 3; in E flat [No. 84] No. 4; in D [No. 86] No. 5; in C [No. 82] No. 6.

On the basis of this information, and taking into consideration the available autographs (which do not contradict Haydn's order), the probable chronological order of the Paris Symphonies should be considerably changed from that given in Mandyczewski's catalogue.

Haydn's autograph of No. 87 is in the *Bibliothèque Nationale*, Paris, catalogue Réserve Vm7 541. As a complete

Joseph Haydn, Symphonie No. 87, A dur

Dieses Werk wurde in E. von Mandyczewskis chronologischer Liste der 104 Symphonien als No. 87 bezeichnet. Als solche stellte es die letzte der Symphonien dar, die Haydn beauftragt war, fuer die Vereinigung "Les Concerts de la Loge Olympique" in Paris zu schreiben. Zu der Zeit, als diese Reihenfolge festgelegt wurde (1907), war das Autograph dieser Symphonie und auch das von No. 83 und 85 der Haydnforschung nicht bekannt. Die spaetere Entdeckung von Haydns eigener Niederschrift von No. 83 und 87 durch Jens Peter Larsen[1] zeigte jedoch, dass Mandyczewskis Reihenfolge der Korrektur bedarf. Es war angenommen worden, dass diese beiden, wie die uebrigen der Serie, von denen Autographe vorhanden waren, 1786 komponiert seien; aber die Autographen von No. 83 und 87 sind beide mit 1785 datiert und demnach vor No. 82, der ersten der 6 Pariser Symphonien in Mandyczewskis Liste, zu stellen. Bei der Eroerterung der Reihenfolge dieser 6 Werke hat, wie es scheint, niemand Haydns diesbezueglichen Brief an seinen Verleger Artaria in Wien beruecksichtigt. In diesem wichtigen Dokument, datiert 2. August 1787, schreibt Haydn[2]:

Ich vergasse letzthin die Ordnung der Sinfonien anzuzeigen, und müssen solche folgenderarth gestochen werden. Die Sinfonia Ex A [G.A. No. 87] Numero 1. Ex b fa [No. 85] Nro 2. Ex g [No. 83] Nro 3. Ex Es [No. 84] Nro 4. Ex D [No. 86] Nro 5. Ex C [No. 82] Nro 6.

Auf Grund dieser Mitteilung und unter Beruecksichtigung der vorhandenen Autographe (die Haydns Reihenfolge nicht widersprechen), muesste die wahrscheinliche chronologische Folge gegenueber Mandyczewskis Katalog erheblich geaendert werden.

Haydns Autograph von No. 87 befindet sich in der *Bibliothèque Nationale*,

description of this source was given by me in the notes to Series I, Volume 9, of the Haydn Society's Complete Edition of the Works of Joseph Haydn, I shall refrain from describing the source here. For that edition, authentic parts by Johann Elssler in the British Museum, London, catalogue Egerton MS. 2379, were also used to establish the text. For this new score by Ernst Eulenburg, Ltd., Haydn's corrected edition, published by Artaria and Co. in Vienna (parts—copy in the *Gesellschaft der Musikfreunde*, Vienna), was also employed. In addition a copy of the work in score, from the Erzherzog Rudolf Collection, also in the *Gesellschaft der Musikfreunde*, was consulted. As compared with the Complete Edition, a few necessary ties and dynamic marks were added in brackets. In the second movement an occasional slur or ornament lacking in the severe critical edition was included here. In the second before last measure of the finale, the autograph has minims in the oboe parts; these were changed to crotchets.

It might be added that the horn parts must, of course, be performed in A *alto*, not, as has occasionally been the unfortunate practice nowadays, in A *basso*. A *basso* is a crook of the horn which was unknown to Haydn (as well as Mozart and Beethoven). It is suggested that, when performing the symphony with large forces, the wind parts be doubled in the *tutti* passages. This is in accordance with Haydn's orchestral practice.[3]

Paris (catalogue Réserve Vm7 541). Da eine genaue Beschreibung dieser Quelle von mir in den Anmerkungen zu Serie I, Band 9 der Ausgabe der Haydn Society gegeben wurde, verzichte ich darauf, diese Beschreibung hier zu wiederholen. Fuer jene Ausgabe wurden zusaetzlich die authentischen Stimmen von Johann Elssler im British Museum, London (catalogue Egerton MS. 2379) benutzt, um den musikalischen Text festzulegen. Fuer die hier vorgelgte Ausgabe der Eulenburg Edition wurde ausserdem die von Haydn selbst korrigierte Ausgabe des Verlages Artaria und Co. (Stimmen) und eine Partiturkopie aus der Erzherzog Rudolf Sammlung (beide Gesellschaft der Musikfreunde, Wien) herangezogen. Gegenueber der Ausgabe der Haydn Society wurden einige notwendige Bindeboegen und dynamische Zeichen in Klammer hinzugefuegt. Im 2. Satz sind gelegentlich ein Bogen oder eine Verzierung, in der streng kritischen Ausgabe fehlend, ergaenzt. Im drittletzten Takt des Finale hat das Autograph in den Oboen halbe Noten; sie wurden in Viertel geaendert.

Zu bemerken ist, dass die Horn-Stimmen natuerlich *A alto* zu blasen sind und nicht, wie es heute zuweilen leider ueblich ist, in *A basso*. Letzteres wuerde einen Bogen fuer das Horn erfordern, der aber Haydn (wie auch Mozart und Beethoven) unbekannt war. Es ist zu empfehlen, bei grosser Besetzung des Orchesters die Blaeser im *Tutti* zu verdoppeln, was auch im Einklang mit Haydns eigener Praxis steht.[3]

H. C. Robbins Landon.

H. C. Robbins Landon.

[1] Jens Peter Larsen, *Die Haydn Uberlieferung*, Copenhagen, 1939, p. 38/39.
[2] Franz Artaria und Hugo Botstiber, *Joseph Haydn und das Verlagshaus Artaria*, Vienna, 1909, p. 50.
[3] It might be pointed out that these symphonies were originally played in Paris with an enormous orchestra, consisting of forty violins and ten double basses, the winds being doubled or even tripled.

[1] Jens Peter Larsen, *Die Haydn-Ueberlieferung* Kopenhagen, 1939, p. 38/9.
[2] Franz Artaria und Hugo Botstiber, *Joseph Haydn und das Verlagshaus Artaria*. Wien, 1909, p. 50.
[3] Es darf darauf hingewiesen werden, dass diese Symphonien urspruenglich in Paris von einem gewaltigen Orchester, bestehend aus 40 Violinen, 10 Baessen und doppelten oder sogar dreifachen Blaesern gespielt wurden.

In Nomine Domini

Sinfonia No. 87

Joseph Haydn
(1732-1809)

I

No. 533   E. E. 6040   Ernst Eulenburg Ltd.

6

8

14

II

22

E. E. 6040

E.E. 6040

28

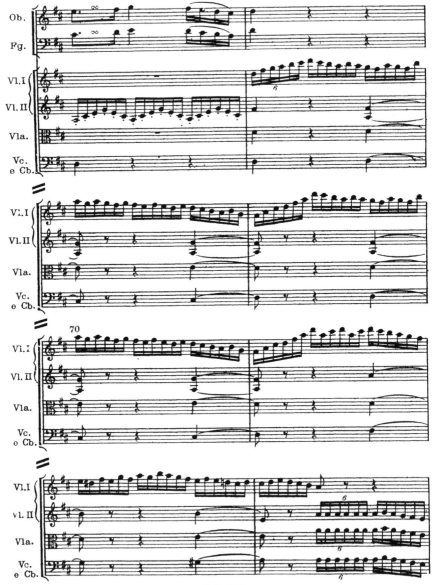

E. E. 6040

E. E. 6040

E. E. 6040

32

E.E. 6040

III

E. E. 6040

34

E. E. 6040

E. E. 6040

Menuet da capo

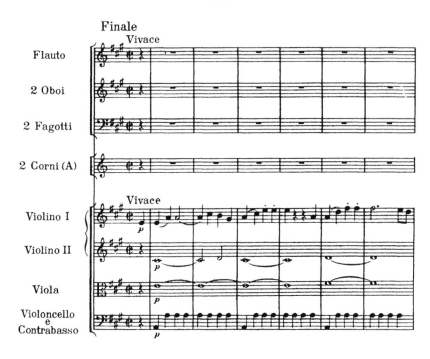

IV

Finale

E. E. 6040